Traffic in Truth

FACETS

The Measure of a Man,
Martin Luther King Jr.

*Visionary Women: Three Medieval
Mystics,* Rosemary Radford Ruether

*The Sayings of Jesus: The Sayings Gospel
Q in English,* James M. Robinson

Spirituality of the Psalms,
Walter Brueggemann

Biblical Theology: A Proposal,
Brevard S. Childs

The Contemporary Quest for Jesus,
N. T. Wright

Christian Faith and Religious Diversity,
Mobilization for the Human Family,
John B. Cobb Jr., editor

Who Is Christ for Us? Dietrich Bonhoeffer

*The Bible and African Americans:
A Brief History,* Vincent L. Wimbush

*Ancient Palestine:
A Historical Introduction,* Gösta Ahlström

Race, Racism, and the Biblical Narratives,
Cain Hope Felder

Traffic in Truth

Exchanges between Science and Theology

John Polkinghorne

Fortress Press
Minneapolis

TRAFFIC IN TRUTH
Exchanges between Science and Theology

First Fortress Press edition, 2002.

Published in collaboration with the Canterbury Press,
Norwich, England.

Cover and book design: Joseph Bonyata
Cover image: Two Trains in Railroad Station photo-
graphed by Mark Purdom © 2002 Photonica. Used by
permission.

0-8006-3579-5

The paper used in this publication meets the minimum
requirements of American National Standard for Information Sciences—Permanence of Paper for Printed Li-
brary Materials, ANSI Z329.48-1984.

Manufactured in the U.S.A.
06 05 04 03 02 1 2 3 4 5 6 7 8 9 10

Contents

)

103532

1

The Frontier

Borders are places of opportunity and of danger, the corridors of trade and the haunts of smugglers and brigands. I have spent twenty years or so as an inhabitant of the intellectual frontier region where the scholarly domains of science and theology meet each other. It has been a lively and interesting place to be, with much cross-border traffic and the occasional border war. People approach this frontier with many different attitudes. Here are some of them:

Denial

Some fail totally to realize that there is territory on the other side. A few of my scientific colleagues think that science is the only real source of knowledge and that the only questions worth asking and answering are those that are scientific in character. There may be talk of a land beyond, but they consider this a fantasy tale, based on unfounded opinion and airy chatter. It is hard to exaggerate the implausibility of this view. The land of science rings with tales of great successes, but that is partly because the inhabitants of that land have set themselves a limited range of tasks to accomplish. They are concerned with asking the question, How do things happen, by what processes do things come about? Their discoveries have taught us many important things about the structure and history of the universe in which we live. Yet there are many other questions that are meaningful and necessary for us to ask—for example, the Why question about whether there is meaning and purpose in what has been going on in cosmic history. That is certainly a harder question to answer than the scientific How question, but it is also even more interesting and we should surely be prepared to tackle it. That will mean venturing over science's frontier into other territory, including into the land of theology. We should not condemn ourselves to thinking that we have said all we can say about music when science has enabled us to note that it is vibrations in the air. We need to recognize also music's mysterious power to use a pattern of sound in time to speak to our hearts of an everlasting beauty. That acknowledgment may well point us in the direction of the Eternal, whose joy in creation is, I believe, the ground of our creaturely aesthetic experience.

It is harder for dwellers in theology-land to pretend that there is no domain of science. Where have our television sets and word processors come from, if not from technological developments that ultimately sprang from science's basic understanding of the workings of the physical world? In the way of producing devices, science impinges upon all of us, but it is possible to avert our eyes from where these conveniences have come from. Some of my theological colleagues seem to dwell in a kind of intellectual ghetto, where answers to deep questions are apparently provided in the form of unquestionable and mysterious information, to which the name of "faith" is misapplied. Of course, theology does have its own sources of insight, but these are not a collection of non-negotiable propositions but the record of God's revelatory acts conveyed through the history of a people (Israel), a person (Jesus Christ), and a community (the church). The God thus made known is the Lord of all creation, and so all forms of rational human inquiry into that creation have something to say to the theologian. He or she has to grapple with the grand task of understanding in order to believe and believing in order to understand. Those who seek to serve the God of truth in this way should welcome truth from whatever quarter it may come. Some of the truth about the rich, many-layered world in which we live comes to us from science. I am a passionate believer in the unity of knowledge, and that belief is underwritten by my belief in the unity of the Creator, who is the ground of all that is. Theology, properly understood, proclaims the border we are discussing to be a free-trade area for the ready exchange of intellectual goods.

Conflict

Borders are where wars begin, and the border between science and theology has sometimes been seen by dwellers on both sides as being a battleground. There is indeed land on the other side, but its fate is to be conquered.

The armies that advance from science-land flourish a banner inscribed "Scientism." It proclaims the triumph of science over all other claims to meaningful insight. Today the bearers of this device are usually biologists. They say: "You think that there are moral imperatives, but *really* they are nothing more than disguised survival strategies, imposed on us by evolution. You think that there is religious experience and insight, but *really* religion is just a helpful delusion, a useful device to keep up our spirits in adversity and to encourage us to struggle on. Human art and cultural achievements are *really* no more than the superficial effects of many molecules interacting with each other. Living organisms are just DNA's way of making more DNA; selfish genes is what it's *really* about."

These kinds of scientistic assertions (usually expressed in a less frank and crude form) can be found in many best-selling popular books about science. It is hard to exaggerate how *unreal* they are. The method is to take direct human experiences (morality, worship, art, encounter with persons) and replace them with abstractified accounts that bear little relation to the quality and character of the experiences themselves. The procedure used is what is called "reductionism": splitting entities into parts and believing that all reality lies in the resulting fragments. The smaller the parts, the more significant the reality is then held to be. (Though—oddly enough—geneticists usually draw the line at genes and don't go on to decompose these complex chemicals into elementary particles such as quarks and gluons and electrons!)

We can learn a lot by using reductionist *techniques* but there are many things we can never learn that way. A chemist might tell us the composition and location of every speck of paint making up the *Mona Lisa,* but the reality of that great painting would have slipped completely through the wide meshes of that chemist's scientific net. Wholes are more than the sum of their parts; paintings are more than assemblages of specks of paint. The reductionist slogan of "Divide and Rule" is a hollow slogan. It can never lead to a real conquest beyond science's border.

It would be nice to be able to say that dwellers on the theological side of the frontier have been wiser than to adopt a misplaced strategy of attempted conquest. Unfortunately, that has not always been the case. A misunderstanding of the nature of the Bible has led some Christians to believe that it contains all necessary truth about pretty well everything. This leads, for example, to the attempt to read Genesis 1 not as a profound assertion of the theological truth that everything exists only because of the will of God ("And God said, let there be . . ."), but as a divinely dictated scientific textbook, saving us trouble by giving us an itemized account of how the universe began. When modern scientific insight differs from this picture (as it mostly does in detail), then the science must be manipulated and made to conform. This attempt at conquest leads to creation science, falsely so-called.

The creationists (in this sense of the word) are trying to annex science's territory and to make it their own. This saddens me for two reasons. One is that they thereby reject much that could speak to them of the grandeur and wonder of God's creation. The other is that, by insisting on such absurdities as a six-thousand-year-old Earth, they discredit Christianity's reputation for truth and seek to bind burdens on believers and inquirers that are too heavy to be borne.

Battlefields are grievous sights. Truth is usually the first casualty of war. If the border between science and theology is perceived as being the launch pad for conquest, it will be a melancholy frontier indeed.

Sealed

Some frontiers are closed and impenetrable. There is a body of opinion that holds that this should apply to the science and theology border.

I have already said that, broadly speaking, science is asking the How questions and theology is asking the Why questions. These are two different kinds of question—should that not then lead to there being two wholly separate kinds of discourse? On this view, inhabitants on both sides of the frontier can simply get on with their own business without bothering about what the others are getting up to or saying to them. It is claimed that we can save ourselves a lot of trouble by simply sealing the border.

This line of argument has appealed to quite a few in both communities. The American National Academy of Science issued a statement a few years ago along just such lines. Effectively they said, "You religious people pay attention to your concerns and we'll pay attention to ours." A little reflection might have enabled the NAS to recognize that quite a few of its members in fact had residences on both sides of the border. Religious believers may not be a majority among professional scientists, but we are certainly pretty numerous.

This kind of live-and-let-live policy has also appealed to some theologians. If "faith" were to be a different kind of knowing from any other form of human knowledge and if "revelation" were to be a matter of propositional certainty rather than particularly transparent experiences of the divine, then theology could get on very nicely without having much to do with science, or any other form of human insight for that matter. I have already declined to live in such a fideistic ghetto. To do so would be to fail to take the doctrine of creation seriously.

A truce between science and religion achieved by sealing the border would be a capitulation to compartmentalism that we should surely reject. How and Why are different questions, but the ways in which we answer them have to fit together and make mutual sense. I might answer your Why question about my purpose for tomorrow by saying that I intend to make a beautiful garden, but if I then go on to answer your How question by saying that my first act will be to cover the ground with six inches of green concrete, you will rightly doubt the truth of my first reply. The two statements were not consonant with each other. Science cannot tell theology how to answer theological questions, and theology cannot tell science how to answer scientific questions, but the two sets of answers will have to fit in with each other if they are really describing the one world of God's creation.

Exchange

The arguments just given imply that theology and science must have things to say to each other. The border between them must be open and there will be fruitful traffic across it in both directions. Science will tell theology what the structure and the history of the physical world are like. Theology will gratefully acknowledge these gifts and seek to set them within the more profound and comprehensive setting that belief in God affords. In its turn, this will enable theology to offer gifts to science that can make more intelligible the success and character of the scientific enterprise. A fruitful exchange is possible between science-land and theology-land. It is to the detailed consideration of this cross-border traffic that we must now turn. We shall start with the export goods that science can offer to theology.

2

Insights from Science

The universe as we know it sprang into being about fifteen billion years ago in the fiery event we call the big bang. The infant universe that then appeared was extremely simple—essentially just an expanding ball of energy. After that fifteen-billion-year history, the world has become very rich and complex, containing galaxies and stars, elephants and people. Science can tell us a great deal about how this has happened. Two complementary insights are fundamental to the story of developing fruitfulness: evolution and fine-tuning.

Evolution

The very early universe was almost as smooth as could be, though by chance there were some little ripples of energy-matter that slightly disturbed that primeval uniformity. If there was initially a little more matter here than there, it would exert a slightly stronger gravitational attraction, pulling that much more matter towards itself. In this way, a kind of snow-balling process started up by which the initial smoothness was increasingly modified and the universe began to become lumpy. After about a billion years or so, the concentrations of matter that we now recognize as galaxies and stars had come into being. As we shall see, this was an essential first step in the dawning fruitfulness of the universe.

This process was an evolving one, resulting from the interplay of two different effects. One might be called "chance," the way in which there just happened to be those small irregularities that were the seeds from which the galaxies began to grow. The other might be called "necessity," the lawfully regular effect of gravity which meant that inevitably a slight excess of matter augmented itself by drawing more matter into a growing lump.

Evolution seems always to involve this interaction between chance and necessity. A more familiar example is the evolution of life here on Earth. By chance, a genetic mutation turns the stream of life in a particular direction. If a different mutation had occurred, the stream would have flowed along a somewhat different path. Chance is the source of novelty, but the offerings of chance are then sifted and preserved in a lawfully regular environment. Evolving fruitfulness seems to require a compromise between reliability and change. Too reliable a world would be so rigid that nothing really new ever took place; too changeable a world would be in such a state of flux that nothing would ever persist in it. Biological evolution requires that genetic inheritance is not absolutely perfect (for otherwise new species could never appear) nor totally unstable (for otherwise species would never become established and subject to natural selection).

Some of the dwellers on the science side of our frontier have seized on the role of chance and asserted that it shows that the theological claim of a creative Purpose at work is just plain wrong. In their view, history is no more than a game of cosmic roulette, and life on Earth just represents a fluky play in that ultimately meaningless game.

The theologian can respond by asking us to look carefully at what "chance" actually means. It does not signify empty randomness but historical particularity. One might rename it "happenstance." This has happened rather than that (this particular ripple of matter, this particular genetic mutation). There is so much possibility present in the world that not everything that could have happened has actually happened. Recognizing this is the rebuttal of the charge of meaninglessness. Instead, one can see evolutionary history as being a kind of shuffling exploration of fertility, bringing to light the deep potentialities of created matter. In a somewhat similar fashion, playing many hands of bridge (but by no means every possible hand) brings to light the potentialities of that subtle game.

Interestingly enough, theologians said something like this from the very start of evolutionary understanding. Darwin's great book, *The Origin of Species,* was published in 1859. Popular myth presents this event as a collision between the scientific forces of light and the religious forces of obscurantist darkness, but this is a travesty of the truth. Some distinguished scientists of the day, including the great comparative anatomist Sir Richard Owen, opposed Darwin's ideas on scientific grounds. Some clergymen welcomed his insights. One of these was Charles Kingsley, who coined a phrase that perfectly expresses the right theological way to think about evolution. The Creator, Kingsley said, could no doubt have brought into being a world ready-made, but instead God has done something cleverer than that in making a creation that could "make itself."

A little reflection shows us how appropriate an action this was for the God of love. Creation could never be just the divine puppet theatre, for the gift of love is always the gift of a due degree of independence to the object of love. (Think of loving parents in relation to the free development of their children.) The role of happenstance can then be understood as the Creator's gift, allowing creation to explore its potentiality and to make itself—just as the regularity of the laws of nature can be understood as signs of God's faithful reliability. In the interplay of chance and necessity, rightly understood, has lain the fruitfulness of creation. In this way, dwellers on the theological side of the border can gratefully accept science's insights about the evolving history of life and of the universe and incorporate them, honestly and helpfully, into the deeper story that theology has to tell.

Indeed, science's gift offers theology modest help with the greatest theological problem of all—the problem of pain and suffering. There is an unavoidable cost involved in a world allowed to make itself. The very same processes that allow cells to mutate and produce new forms of life will inevitably allow other cells to mutate and become malignant. The fact that there is cancer in creation is not due to divine callousness or incompetence; it is the inescapable dark side of the good of an evolving creation.

Fine-Tuning

Scientific study of the history of the universe has made it plain that the evolutionary explorations of chance are only a part of the story that links a ball of energy to a world containing human beings. The necessity, or lawfully ordered side of the process, has played a particularly significant role as well. If the laws of nature had not been what they actually are, there would have been no deep potentiality for happenstance to explore. The physical fabric of the universe had to be "finely-tuned" to the possibility of carbon-based life from the very start. We live in a very special world and beings like ourselves could not have appeared in just any old universe.

This discovery is usually called the Anthropic Principle: a universe capable of evolving *anthrōpoi* (Greek for human beings) is a very special universe indeed. Of course, by referring to *anthrōpoi* one does not mean to suggest that human beings (with five fingers, etc.) were implied from the start. Rather it is some sort of beings of our general complexity that are intended, capable of being consciously aware of themselves. The Anthropic Principle came as a great surprise to dwellers in science-land. They prefer to talk in as general terms as possible and so their natural instinct was to suppose that our universe was nothing very special among possible worlds. They had not at all anticipated that there would be something of unique significance in the precise form taken by our laws of nature.

To understand what this surprising particularity is all about, consider a universe that was almost exactly the same as ours in its physical constitution, but with just one small change. All its laws of nature are just like ours except that gravity in that world is three times stronger. One might well have expected that such a universe would eventually evolve its own form of life. Of course, it wouldn't be *Homo sapiens*. It would be something different—little green men, maybe. (And they would be expected to be little, since stronger gravity would make it harder to grow tall.) Actually, there would be no inhabitants of that universe at all. Its history would be boring and sterile; the interplay of chance with its necessity would never bring anything interesting to birth. What would have gone wrong? The stars in that world would not be the right sort of stars, capable of fuelling the development of life on one of its planets. Life has been able to evolve here on Earth because our local star, the Sun, has been shining for five billion years or so, supplying energy for the four-billion-year history of terrestrial life. In that other universe, the stars would burn very much more brightly and so exhaust their energy supplies very much more quickly. The change in gravity would have the effect that after only a few million years they would all be burnt out. Those stars would not be around anything like long enough to enable carbon-based life to get going.

The more one thinks about the plot of life, the more that plot thickens. Stars in our universe have played a second essential role in enabling life to develop. The chemistry of life is the chemistry of carbon. Every atom of carbon in our bodies was once inside a star—it's the only place where carbon can be produced. We are all made from the ashes of dead stars. In fact, almost all the chemical raw materials of life come from star dust. The way these essential elements are made in the stellar nuclear furnaces is through a very delicate chain of reactions. The slightest change in the nature of the basic nuclear forces would sever some of the links in that chain. One of the scientists who played a major role in working out the wonderful tale of how the stars make the chemical elements was Fred Hoyle. When he saw the delicacy of the fine-tuning that had made this possible, he was moved to say that the universe is a "put-up job." This could not be just a happy accident; there must be some Intelligence behind it all.

Many more examples could be given of how special our universe has been found to be. One final illustration must suffice. We live in a world that is immensely big: a hundred billion galaxies, each with a hundred billion stars. Sometime we may feel upset by the thought of such immensity. It makes us feel that we are just dwellers on a speck of cosmic dust. What possible significance could there be to that? Well, we should not feel that way, for if all those trillions of stars were not there, we would not be here to be upset at them. Only a universe as big as ours could last the fifteen billion years it takes to make men and women. Even the gigantic size of the universe is an anthropic necessity.

We will defer considering further what significance might be attributed to these remarkable discoveries until we can draw the inhabitants of theology-land into the conversation.

Death of Mechanism

The great discoveries of Sir Isaac Newton seemed to lead to a scientific picture of physical process as being predictable and mechanical. The universe appeared to be a gigantic piece of clockwork, with God reduced to the role of a cosmic Clockmaker. There was always something fishy about this, since we surely know that we ourselves are not mere automata. Twentieth-century science, in fact, saw the death of this mechanical account of the universe. Nature was found to be full of intrinsic unpredictabilities.

The first discovery revealing that this is so was quantum theory. Study of processes on the scale of atoms or smaller forced physicists, slowly and reluctantly, to the recognition that at the subatomic roots of the world all is cloudy and fitful. It is well known that quantum theory does not deal in predictable certainties but only in probabilities. We may be able to say that half of the atoms in a lump of radioactive material will decay in the next hour, but we are quite unable to say which individual atoms will decay in this way and which will not.

Important—indeed, startling—as this discovery was, these uncertainties seldom directly affect processes on a scale big enough for us to be aware of them, for these involve trillions upon trillions of atomic interactions. In a large collection of random events, the uncertainties of individual behavior tend to cancel each other out to give an overall regularity of the whole. It is rather like life insurance. The actuaries do not know when you are going to die, but if they can insure a sufficient number of people of your ages they can predict what fraction will die in the next five years with sufficient accuracy to be able to make money.

In the last forty years, however, a second source of unpredictability has come to light. It is present in processes taking place at any everyday level of which we are easily aware. It turns out that these events are by no means all as tame and controllable as Newton and his successors had led us to believe. This insight is called "chaos theory." There are clocks around, but most complex systems turn out to be "clouds." By that I mean that they are so exquisitely sensitive to the details of their circumstances that the slightest nudge will produce totally changed future behavior. It will come as no surprise that one of the areas in which this realization first dawned was that of attempting to understand the weather. It is a kind of serious joke to call this extreme sensitivity "the butterfly effect." In certain circumstances, the Earth's weather systems are so sensitive that a butterfly in the African jungle, stirring the air with its wings today, could produce consequences that grow and grow until they produce a storm thousands of miles away over our heads in about three weeks time. Long-term weather forecasting is never going to work; we shall never be able to keep track of all those African butterflies!

That there are these two sources of physical uncertainty—quantum theory and chaos theory—is an accepted fact. There is, however, still much debate about what wider implications might follow from that. Is it no more than an acceptance that we are condemned to an unfortunate degree of ignorance about what is going to happen, or is it a sign that in fact there is an actual openness about what is going to happen? Is that openness the way in which we are delivered from being automata and instead are able to act as agents, bringing about our willed intentions for the future? Is that openness also the way in which God interacts with creation, providing the channel through which divine providence is ceaselessly at work, guiding and leading creatures? The debate rolls on, but I personally would answer these questions affirmatively. Certainly, I think we can say that contemporary science offers theology the opportunity for a more congenial picture of physical process than it did in previous centuries.

There is another way in which this is so, also resulting from study of the behavior of complex systems. This sort of research has only recently become possible. Previously it was too difficult, but now the power of modern computers enables us to investigate some very complicated models. When this is done, it is found that such systems are often capable of spontaneously generating astonishing patterns displaying high degrees of order. It seems that the behavior of these systems needs for its full description not just the familiar ideas of interchanges of energy between their parts, but also a concept of pattern-forming information that orders the whole. Centuries ago, the great medieval theologian Thomas Aquinas suggested that we should think of the human soul as the "form" (that is, the almost infinitely complex pattern) of the body. Modern science certainly seems to be pointing us again in that direction. Theologians can then use this idea to make sense of the Christian hope of a resurrected human destiny beyond death. It can be pictured as being the result of God's remembering the individual patterns that we are and reconstituting them again in the life of the world to come.

How Will It End?

Scientists not only peer into the past of the universe. They can also look into its future. On the biggest possible scale, cosmic history is a gigantic tug-of-war between two finely balanced and opposing tendencies. One is the fiery explosion of the big bang driving matter apart. We see its effect in the presently observed expansion of the universe. The other is the pull of gravity, ceaselessly acting to draw matter together. We are unable to be sure which will win in the end, and so there are two alternative scenarios for the cosmic future. If expansion wins, the galaxies will continue to recede from each other forever. Within themselves they will eventually collapse and decay. That way, the world will end in a whimper. On the other hand, if gravity wins, the present expansion will one day be halted and reversed. What began with the big bang will then end in the big crunch, as the whole universe falls back into a fiery melting pot. That way, the world ends with a bang.

Either way, the universe is condemned to ultimate futility. It will not happen for billions of years, but one or the other of these fates will eventually overtake the cosmos. Carbon-based life may continue to flourish for billions of years longer, but in the end all will be lifeless again. This gloomy prediction is one that theologians have to take seriously and we shall see in due course what they make of it.

3

Insights from Theology

Theology is not in a position to tell science what to think about its own proper concerns. That would be to try to turn science-land into a colony of theology-land, the kind of mistake that led the church into the errors committed in the course of the Galileo affair. One god who is well and truly dead is the god of gaps. He was invoked as the explanation, so-called, of current gaps in scientific knowledge. We have learned, however, not to make statements like "Only the direct intervention of God could have produced the complexity of the human eye." Darwin gave us the possibility of an alternative explanation. We have come to expect that scientifically posable questions will receive scientifically stateable answers, however difficult those answers may sometimes be to find. No one should shed a tear about this since the god of the gaps was only a pseudo-deity anyway. He faded

away with every advance of knowledge,
like a kind of divine Cheshire cat. The true
God, the Creator, is related to the whole of
creation, not just the bits that are hard to
understand. Theology's job is not to rival
science on its own ground (the How questions) but to *complement* science by offering its own more profound kind of
understanding (the answers to Why questions). We must now consider some of the
offerings that theologians can convey
across the frontier to science-land.

Intelligibility

We can begin by posing a question that
people seldom stop to ask but that is very
well worth considering. It is simply, "Why
is science possible at all? Why can we understand the universe so profoundly?"

Of course, we must have a rough and
ready understanding of everyday occurrences in order to be able to survive. If we
could not make generalizations such as "It
is a bad idea to step off the top of a high
cliff," we would not be around for very
long. But it by no means follows from this
that someone with the genius of Isaac

Newton could come along and by an astonishing creative leap of the human imagination see that the same force that made the cliff dangerous was also the force that held the moon in its orbit around the Earth, and the Earth in its orbit around the sun, and through that realization to discover universal inverse-square law gravitation and explain the workings of the whole solar system.

Something is involved here that goes far beyond the need for survival. When Sherlock Holmes and Dr. Watson first met, the detective pulled the leg of the medical man by pretending not to know whether the Earth went around the sun or the sun went around the Earth. In response to Watson's horror at this ignorance, Holmes simply said, "What does it matter for my life as a detective?" Of course, it did not, but human powers of understanding go far beyond mundane necessity.

In fact the matter is stranger still, for it is *mathematics* that is the key to unlocking the secrets of the physical universe. It is an actual technique in fundamental physics to look for theories that are elegant and economic in their mathematical expression because it has been our repeated experience that it is only such theories with these qualities of mathematical beauty that convince us of their validity through their long-term fruitfulness in explaining physical phenomena. The search for a beautiful equation was the way in which Albert Einstein discovered general relativity, the modern successor to Newton's theory of gravity. If you have a friend who is a theoretical physicist and you want to upset him or her, just say, "That latest theory of yours looks rather ugly to me."

When we use beautiful mathematics in this way, as a tool for physical discovery, something very odd is happening. After all, what is math? It is the free exploration by human minds of patterns of abstract order. What is it that links these ideas, formed in the study, with the way the universe actually is? It seems too intellectually lazy just to shrug our shoulders and say, "That's just the way it is—and a bit of good luck for you people who are good at math." So deep a fact about the world should not be brushed off as a happy accident. It is something we should try to understand. So, why is the universe so intelligible and rationally beautiful?

Such a profound question cannot be given a knockdown answer, but theology can provide an intellectually satisfying and coherent response. Science is possible, and mathematics is so remarkably effective, because the world is a creation and we are creatures made in the image of the Creator. Fundamental physics reveals a universe shot through with signs of mind, and it is an attractive understanding that it is indeed the Mind of God that lies behind that wonderful cosmic order.

The Anthropic Principle

The fine-tuning of the laws of nature, which alone has enabled the evolution of carbon-based life, is another scientific discovery that it would be totally inadequate to consider as just a happy accident. A philosopher who has thought about these matters is John Leslie and in his book, *Universe,* he puts the issue before us by telling a story:

You are about to be executed. You are tied to the stake and the rifles of ten highly trained marksmen are leveled at your chest. The officer gives the order to fire and the shots ring out . . . You find you have survived!

What do you do? Do you just shrug your shoulders and walk away, saying "That was a close one"? Of course not. So remarkable an occurrence demands an explanation. Leslie suggests there are only two rational explanations of your good fortune:

(a) Maybe many, many executions are taking place today. Even the best of marksmen sometimes miss and you happen to be in the execution where they all miss. Of course there would really have to be a vast number of executions scheduled today to make this a plausible explanation, but if there were enough going on this would be a conceivable way of accounting for your escape.

(b) Maybe there is only one execution scheduled today, namely yours. However, more was going on in that event than you had realized. The marksmen were on your side. They missed by design.

One sees how this charming parable translates into thinking about anthropic fine-tuning. First, we should seek an explanation. It is not enough to say, "We're here because we're here, and that's that."

Basically there are two possibilities. Maybe there are many, many separate universes, all different, with different physical laws and circumstances. If there are enough— and again there would have to be a truly vast number—then one of them will, by chance, fulfill the conditions for carbon-based life. That, of course, is the universe in which we live, because we could not appear in the history of any other. Alternatively, maybe there is only one universe, which is the way it is because it is not just any old world but it is a creation which has been endowed by its Creator with precisely those natural laws that will enable it to have a fruitful history.

Which of these two explanations should we choose? Leslie suggests that it is a fifty-fifty choice; either option in itself is equally plausible in his opinion. Citizens of science-land who wish to have nothing to do with what happens on the other side of the border will have to opt for the many-universes explanation. They may even think that they are speaking the language of science in doing so, but that is not the case. We only have direct scientific motivation to speak of the one universe of our actual experience. Those talking of lots of other universes are making a metaphysical guess that goes beyond science itself. Equally, of course, it is a metaphysical guess, in the same sense, to talk of the Creator. That option will be the one that those of us who speak the language of theology will want to take. We can defend our choice in a rational way. Supposing that there are many other universes is a guess that seems to be made simply to finesse the particularity of this finely-tuned world. It does not seem to perform any other useful work. However, the supposition that there is God the Creator not only offers an explanation of anthropic fine-tuning but also does many other useful pieces of explanatory work. For example, we have already seen how it can explain the deep intelligibility of the universe and it would also, of course, explain the basis for understanding the widespread human testimony to experiences that mediate an encounter with the sacred.

Religious Experience

This last point draws our attention to the fact that modern Western agnosticism and atheism present a considerable anomaly in historical and geographical terms. Most people at most times and in most places have had religious beliefs. There is a considerable body of experience of a personal and transpersonal kind (and so lying outside the self-limited impersonal purview of science) to which dwellers in theology-land can appeal. The discussion and evaluation of this material is an enormous task, and here we can no more give an adequate account of it than we have been able to give an adequate account of the vast range of scientific understanding. In each case we have to confine ourselves to those features of the two domains that lie closest to their common frontier. It must suffice for the present to make three points:

1. When theology-land is considered worldwide, it appears to be a country in which many diverse languages are being spoken. This is in striking contrast to the situation on the other side of the border. Ask a suitable person in London, Delhi, or Tokyo to tell you what matter is made of, and you can expect to receive the same answer in all three cities. Ask someone suitable in the same three cities to tell you what is the nature of Ultimate Reality, and

the chances are you will receive three very different responses.

2. Nevertheless, people in all three cities will be witnessing to a common claim of encounter with the sacred, and they will all recognize the reality of a spiritual dimension to life that transcends the merely physical. There is some kind of underlying linkage of the diverse languages of theology-land. For example, Christianity and Zen Buddhism are two very different religions, but monks and nuns from both communities can acknowledge the spiritual authenticity present in the lives of those from the other tradition.

3. Yet we cannot claim that all religions are really saying the same thing, although in culturally different ways. There are real clashes of understanding. Some of these involve the status of key figures, as when Muslims respect Jesus as one of God's prophets but repudiate the central Christian claim that he is the Son of God. Other clashes can involve such issues as disagreements about the status of the human being. The Abrahamic faiths (Judaism, Christianity, and Islam) all see each human person as having a unique and enduring status, derived from the steadfast love of

the Creator for individuals; Hinduism believes that persons are recycled through
reincarnation; the Buddhist doctrine of
anatta proclaims the concept of the self to
be an illusion from which we are to seek
release. No easy reconciliation of these
views is possible.

Many perplexities arise from the diversity of theological discourse. The continu-
ing discussion of these problems is one of
the most important items on the contemporary theological agenda. It may be that
looking across the border toward science,
and discussing together the nature of the
traffic across that frontier, will provide a
relatively non-threatening way in which
the great world faith traditions may begin
to explore their mutual encounter.

The Futility of the Universe

Theologians have to take seriously science's
prognostications of the ultimate fate of the
universe. That insight, in fact, does not
seem to present theology with a challenge
all that different from that raised by the
even more certain knowledge of our own
individual apparent futility on a time scale
of tens of years. Death, whether it is the

death of the universe or the death of a person, places a question mark over the Creator's intentions for the fulfillment of creation.

Science rules out a merely evolutionary optimism—the idea that present process will lead to ultimate fulfillment—but theology responds by pointing to the faithfulness of God as the only true ground of an everlasting hope. This is exactly the point that Jesus made in his argument with the Sadducees about whether there is a human destiny beyond death (Mark 12:18-27). He reminded them that God is the God of Abraham, Isaac, and Jacob, "God not of the dead, but of the living." In other words, if the patriarchs mattered to God once, as they most certainly did, then they must matter to God forever. If any part of creation matters to God—and surely the Creator cares appropriately for every part of creation—then it will matter to God forever. Christianity has never tried to avoid recognizing the reality of death, but it has always sought to look beyond that to the greater reality of God's act of resurrection.

Christian hope believes that the foretaste and guarantee of that divine faithfulness has already been given us in the resurrection of Jesus Christ. The empty tomb, with its message that the Lord's risen body is the transmuted and glorified form of his dead body, speaks of a destiny in Christ for *matter* as well as humanity. The remarkable first chapter of the epistle to the Colossians paints a portrait of the Cosmic Christ, the one who has redeemed "all things [not just all people]" (Col. 1:20). These are mysterious and exciting theological insights that are an essential part of a coherent Christian belief.

4

Common Cause

If there is to be traffic across the frontier, the citizens on both sides must attain some kind of respectful relationship with each other. They will retain their "national" identities, but there will have to be some degree of common cause accessible to them if the project of cross-border trading is to seem a worthwhile commitment to pursue.

We have already identified a number of important things scientists can say that are of significance to theologians, and things theologians can say that are of significance to scientists. There remains the question of whether they can have a sufficient degree of mutual confidence, and a sufficiently cousinly way of thinking, to make the exchange a real possibility.

Reason and Revelation

Many people seem to think that science and theology are chalk and cheese, the one concerned with facts and the other dealing only in opinions. Such a view makes two bad mistakes, one about the nature of science and the other about the nature of theology.

Let us take science first. There are no interesting scientific facts that are not already interpreted facts. Experiment and theory (fact and opinion, one might say) are inextricably intertwined. It is only by using current theoretical ideas that we can understand what it is our apparatus might actually be measuring. Modern philosophy of science has recognized that this is so and that it introduces an inevitable degree of circularity into scientific discussion. There is a mutually supportive interchange between experimental observations and their interpretation in terms of theoretical ideas. Although this circularity might seem to make scientific insight somewhat precarious, the cumulative success of science (atoms have come to stay!) suggests strongly that the circularity is benign and not vicious. Science affords us reliable knowledge, but it does not do so by being utterly unlike many other forms of human understanding (including theology), which also have to maintain an interactive balance between experience and understanding.

Theology, in its turn, has long been acquainted with this kind of benign circularity. Theologians know that they must believe in order to understand and understand in order to believe. The claims of theology are not the expressions of prejudiced opinion, but theologians have motivations for their beliefs. Reason has a role to play in both science and theology. Revelation is not some set of propositions, derived in an ineffable manner and presented for the unquestioning acceptance of the faithful on the basis of an unchallengeable authority. Rather, revelation is the record of those events in which the divine presence and nature have been made most clearly discernible. Scripture is not a divinely dictated infallible book, but the inspired human record of these foundational revelatory events.

In fact, revelation plays a similar role in theology to that played by experiments and observations in science. The laws of nature are always operating, but there are certain events in which their workings can most clearly be discerned. We call these events experiments. Such special occasions are brought about by clever human contrivance. Similarly, God is always present and at work, but there are particular happenings in which the divine is most clearly perceivable. We call that revelation. However, these theologically significant special occasions cannot be brought about by human contrivance; they must be accepted as gracious divine gift.

Miracle

Yet among these revelatory events are those that are claimed to be totally different from common human experience. We call these events "miracles," and central to Christian belief is the miracle of the resurrection of Jesus Christ. It is the hinge on which such belief turns, for without it the story of Jesus is strangely ambiguous in its significance. Alone among the great religious leaders of world history, Jesus dies, not in honored old age surrounded by disciples resolved to continue the work of the master, but painfully and shamefully executed in mid-life, deserted by his followers. It seems like an ending in total failure. In fact, I believe that if that had been the end of the Jesus story, we would never have heard of him. He wrote no book and he would just have disappeared from history. But we all have heard of him, and so something must have happened to continue the story of Jesus beyond his death. I believe the Christian claim that that "something" was God's raising Jesus the first Easter Day.

But how could theologians make that belief intelligible to interested visitors from science-land? Has not science shown us how regular and orderly the world is and that as part of that order, dead men stay dead? Actually, the real problem of miracle is not scientific but theological. What is *theologically* incredible is that God would ever act like a show-off celestial conjurer, doing a turn today to astonish people that God did not think of doing yesterday and will not be bothered to do tomorrow. The God whose faithful will lies behind the regularities of created nature is not condemned never to do anything new and unexpected, but we can anticipate that these new acts will be understandable as signs of a deeper aspect of the divine nature than had been manifested before. In other words, the problem of miracle is the problem of divine consistency. Putting it bluntly, miracles have to make theological sense if they are to be credible. The resurrection seems to me wholly to satisfy this criterion. It makes sense because it vindicates Jesus (whose story should not have ended in failure); it vindicates God (who did not abandon the one person who wholly committed himself to the divine will); it vindicates human hope that death does not have the last word in any of our stories. Remember that in Christian understanding, what is special about Jesus' resurrection is not so much that it happened as when it happened. It is the foretaste and guarantee, enacted within history, of a destiny awaiting the rest of us beyond history. "For as in Adam all die, so also in Christ shall all be made alive" (1 Cor. 15:22).

Truth

Both science and theology believe that there is a truth to be found, or more accurately to be approximated. Much contemporary thinking has given up the search for truth and believes that there is nothing but a cultural variety of human opinions, from which we can make our *à la carte* choice but between which we cannot make

a decisive judgment. (This cultural rela-
tivism is often called "postmodernism.")
Neither scientists nor theologians are will-
ing to succumb to this intellectual pes-
simism.

Of course, we shall never know *all* there
is to know about the physical world. It is
too rich a reality for that. But through science we are able to gain an increasingly
tightening grip on its nature. Even more,
finite human minds will never attain *full*
understanding of the infinite mystery of
God. No doubt this mismatch of human
finitude and divine infinity is one reason
why theology is so much less successful in
reaching universally agreed answers to its
questions, in contrast to science's impres-
sive power to settle issues to general satis-
faction. Nevertheless, there is a cousinly
connection between the dwellers in science-land and the dwellers in theology-
land. Their common cause for truth means
that the frontier between them will always
be busy with traffic across its open border.
For both sides, the question of truth is the
paramount question.

One further important cousinly connection between the two groups of people is

that both are led to belief in unseen realities. As a particle physicist I am completely convinced of the existence of quarks and gluons, the most basic constituents of matter that currently are known to us. Yet I have never seen one of them and if contemporary ideas are correct, no one ever will. We believe that these entities are so tightly bound within nuclear matter that no impact will ever be energetic enough to eject one. Why then am I and my colleagues so convinced of their existence? The answer is that this belief makes sense of great swathes of physical experience that otherwise it would be very difficult to understand. It is the intelligibility that belief in quarks confers that persuades us of their reality. It is much the same for my belief in the unseen reality of God. That belief makes sense of great swathes of human experience, from considering the wonderful fine-tuning of the universe to my encounter with the figure of Jesus Christ as I meet him in Scripture, the sacraments, and the church.

5

A Long Frontier

I am a person who spends a lot of time inhabiting part of the borderland we have been visiting. I have tramped many times across the boundary and found a helpful and happy lodging on both its sides. However, I have only been able to explore a small part of that long frontier.

My scientific experience lies in physics, and it will not have escaped the reader's notice that much of the material we have considered together has had its origin in physical science. That particular part of the border has been crossed by many travelers. Physics is a comparatively easy subject when compared with the complexities that face those who study life. Even more so is that true of the comparison with those who study human nature. Physics is in many ways a mature subject, and in its study both of the very small (quantum theory) and the very large (cosmology) it has encountered the sort of intellectual frontier along which what may be called "limit questions" (arising from scientific insight and experience but going beyond the merely scientific) naturally arise. We have seen that these limit questions (intelligibility, fine-tuning) can quite naturally lead to answers that serve as hints and rumors of a divine mind behind the rational order of the universe and a divine purpose behind its fertile history. They are signposts pointing across to theology-land.

Our explorations took us a little way into the biological sector of the border, when we thought about evolution and what it might imply for the theological doctrine of creation. There are many other issues on this part of the frontier, but to explore them you will need another kind of guide. Even further along the border lies the sector of the human sciences, psychology and anthropology. It would be hard to exaggerate the importance of this sector for theology, with that discipline's concern for the human person understood as a creature in the presence of a loving Creator. A very great deal of work needs to be done in this area, much of which is unmapped even by the experts. When we look at cosmic history from the big bang to the present day, perhaps the most surprising, and I believe the most significant, thing that has happened that we know about has been the dawning of self-consciousness on planet Earth. In ourselves, and in our hominid ancestors, the universe has become aware of itself. Blaise Pascal said that human beings are just reeds (insubstantial entities in a vast universe), but we are *thinking* reeds and that makes us greater than all the stars, for we know them and ourselves and they know nothing.

At present consciousness is a deep mystery to science. Yet it is the basis of all human knowledge, including science. Neuroscientists are learning many important things about the pathways in the brain that process information coming to us from the environment. However, there is a yawning chasm between this kind of talk, about neurons and synapses (significant and interesting as that talk is), and the simplest mental experiences, such as toothache or seeing blue. We simply have no idea how to bridge that chasm. Perhaps one day we will do so. I have no desire to rejoice at human ignorance, but it is also possible that we will never be able to stand outside ourselves to understand ourselves, in the way that we can gain understanding of the world around us, which we transcend. Whatever may prove to be the case, in their efforts to understand the nature of humanity, science and theology should stand alongside each other and encourage the greatest possible degree of exchange across their common border.